Baseball Training Log and Diary

This Book Belongs To:

_____

Visit http://elegantnotebooks.com for more
sports training books.

Training Log and Diary
Nutrition Log and Diary
Strength and Conditioning Log and Diary

©Elegant Notebooks

DATE:		WEEK:		HOURS TRAINED:	
INSTRUCTOR:				TIME:	

GOALS

WARM UP/ DRILLS

TECHNIQUE 1

TECHNIQUE 2

NOTES

DATE: **WEEK:**   **HOURS TRAINED:**

INSTRUCTOR: **TIME:**

GOALS

WARM UP/ DRILLS

TECHNIQUE 1

TECHNIQUE 2

NOTES

DATE: _____ **WEEK:** _____ **HOURS TRAINED:** _____

INSTRUCTOR: _____ **TIME:** _____

GOALS

WARM UP/ DRILLS

TECHNIQUE 1

TECHNIQUE 2

NOTES

DATE: _____ **WEEK:** _____ **HOURS TRAINED:** _____

INSTRUCTOR: _____ **TIME:** _____

GOALS

WARM UP/ DRILLS

TECHNIQUE 1

TECHNIQUE 2

NOTES

DATE: _____ **WEEK:** _____ **HOURS TRAINED:** _____

INSTRUCTOR: _____ **TIME:** _____

GOALS

WARM UP/ DRILLS

TECHNIQUE 1

TECHNIQUE 2

NOTES

DATE: _____ **WEEK:** _____ **HOURS TRAINED:** _____

INSTRUCTOR: _____ **TIME:** _____

GOALS

WARM UP/ DRILLS

TECHNIQUE 1

TECHNIQUE 2

NOTES

DATE: [ ] **WEEK:** [ ] **HOURS TRAINED:** [ ]

INSTRUCTOR: [ ] **TIME:** [ ]

GOALS

WARM UP/ DRILLS

TECHNIQUE 1

TECHNIQUE 2

NOTES

DATE: | **WEEK:** | **HOURS TRAINED:**

INSTRUCTOR: | **TIME:**

GOALS

WARM UP/ DRILLS

TECHNIQUE 1

TECHNIQUE 2

NOTES

DATE: _____ **WEEK:** _____ **HOURS TRAINED:** _____

INSTRUCTOR: _____ **TIME:** _____

GOALS

WARM UP/ DRILLS

TECHNIQUE 1

TECHNIQUE 2

NOTES

DATE: _____   **WEEK:** _____   **HOURS TRAINED:** _____

INSTRUCTOR: _____   **TIME:** _____

GOALS

WARM UP/ DRILLS

TECHNIQUE 1

TECHNIQUE 2

NOTES

DATE: _____ **WEEK:** _____ **HOURS TRAINED:** _____

INSTRUCTOR: _____ **TIME:** _____

GOALS

WARM UP/ DRILLS

TECHNIQUE 1

TECHNIQUE 2

NOTES

DATE: **WEEK:** **HOURS TRAINED:**

INSTRUCTOR: **TIME:**

GOALS

WARM UP/ DRILLS

TECHNIQUE 1

TECHNIQUE 2

NOTES

DATE: [ ] **WEEK:** [ ] **HOURS TRAINED:** [ ]

INSTRUCTOR: [ ] **TIME:** [ ]

GOALS

WARM UP/ DRILLS

TECHNIQUE 1

TECHNIQUE 2

NOTES

DATE: **WEEK:** **HOURS TRAINED:**

INSTRUCTOR: **TIME:**

GOALS

WARM UP/ DRILLS

TECHNIQUE 1

TECHNIQUE 2

NOTES

DATE:		WEEK:		HOURS TRAINED:	
INSTRUCTOR:				TIME:	

GOALS

WARM UP/ DRILLS

TECHNIQUE 1

TECHNIQUE 2

NOTES

DATE: _____ **WEEK:** _____ **HOURS TRAINED:** _____

INSTRUCTOR: _____ **TIME:** _____

GOALS

WARM UP/ DRILLS

TECHNIQUE 1

TECHNIQUE 2

NOTES

DATE: _____ **WEEK:** _____ **HOURS TRAINED:** _____

INSTRUCTOR: _____ **TIME:** _____

GOALS

WARM UP/ DRILLS

TECHNIQUE 1

TECHNIQUE 2

NOTES

DATE: _____ **WEEK:** _____ **HOURS TRAINED:** _____

INSTRUCTOR: _____ **TIME:** _____

GOALS

WARM UP/ DRILLS

TECHNIQUE 1

TECHNIQUE 2

NOTES

DATE: **WEEK:** **HOURS TRAINED:**

INSTRUCTOR: **TIME:**

GOALS

WARM UP/ DRILLS

TECHNIQUE 1

TECHNIQUE 2

NOTES

DATE: _____ **WEEK:** _____ **HOURS TRAINED:** _____

INSTRUCTOR: _____ **TIME:** _____

GOALS

WARM UP/ DRILLS

TECHNIQUE 1

TECHNIQUE 2

NOTES

DATE:		WEEK:		HOURS TRAINED:	
INSTRUCTOR:				TIME:	

GOALS

WARM UP/ DRILLS

TECHNIQUE 1

TECHNIQUE 2

NOTES

DATE: **WEEK:**   **HOURS TRAINED:**

INSTRUCTOR: **TIME:**

GOALS

WARM UP/ DRILLS

TECHNIQUE 1

TECHNIQUE 2

NOTES

DATE: _____   **WEEK:** _____   **HOURS TRAINED:** _____

INSTRUCTOR: _____   **TIME:** _____

GOALS

WARM UP/ DRILLS

TECHNIQUE 1

TECHNIQUE 2

NOTES

DATE: [_____] **WEEK:** [_____] **HOURS TRAINED:** [_____]

INSTRUCTOR: [_____] **TIME:** [_____]

GOALS

WARM UP/ DRILLS

TECHNIQUE 1

TECHNIQUE 2

NOTES

DATE: _____ **WEEK:** ____ **HOURS TRAINED:** _____

INSTRUCTOR: _____ **TIME:** _____

GOALS

WARM UP/ DRILLS

TECHNIQUE 1

TECHNIQUE 2

NOTES

DATE: [ ] **WEEK:** [ ] **HOURS TRAINED:** [ ]

INSTRUCTOR: [ ] **TIME:** [ ]

GOALS

WARM UP/ DRILLS

TECHNIQUE 1

TECHNIQUE 2

NOTES

DATE: _____ **WEEK:** _____ **HOURS TRAINED:** _____

INSTRUCTOR: _____ **TIME:** _____

GOALS

WARM UP/ DRILLS

TECHNIQUE 1

TECHNIQUE 2

NOTES

DATE: **WEEK:**   **HOURS TRAINED:**

INSTRUCTOR: **TIME:**

GOALS

WARM UP/ DRILLS

TECHNIQUE 1

TECHNIQUE 2

NOTES

DATE:		WEEK:		HOURS TRAINED:	
INSTRUCTOR:				TIME:	

GOALS

WARM UP/ DRILLS

TECHNIQUE 1

TECHNIQUE 2

NOTES

DATE: [   ] **WEEK:** [   ] **HOURS TRAINED:** [   ]

INSTRUCTOR: [   ] **TIME:** [   ]

GOALS

WARM UP/ DRILLS

TECHNIQUE 1

TECHNIQUE 2

NOTES

DATE: **WEEK:** **HOURS TRAINED:**

INSTRUCTOR: **TIME:**

GOALS

WARM UP/ DRILLS

TECHNIQUE 1

TECHNIQUE 2

NOTES

DATE: _____ **WEEK:** _____ **HOURS TRAINED:** _____

INSTRUCTOR: _____ **TIME:** _____

GOALS

WARM UP/ DRILLS

TECHNIQUE 1

TECHNIQUE 2

NOTES

DATE: _____ **WEEK:** ____ **HOURS TRAINED:** _____

INSTRUCTOR: _____ **TIME:** _____

GOALS

WARM UP/ DRILLS

TECHNIQUE 1

TECHNIQUE 2

NOTES

DATE: _____ **WEEK:** _____ **HOURS TRAINED:** _____

INSTRUCTOR: _____ **TIME:** _____

GOALS

WARM UP/ DRILLS

TECHNIQUE 1

TECHNIQUE 2

NOTES

DATE: _____ **WEEK:** _____ **HOURS TRAINED:** _____

INSTRUCTOR: _____ **TIME:** _____

GOALS

WARM UP/ DRILLS

TECHNIQUE 1

TECHNIQUE 2

NOTES

DATE: **WEEK:** **HOURS TRAINED:**

INSTRUCTOR: **TIME:**

GOALS

WARM UP/ DRILLS

TECHNIQUE 1

TECHNIQUE 2

NOTES

DATE: **WEEK:**   **HOURS TRAINED:**

INSTRUCTOR: **TIME:**

GOALS

WARM UP/ DRILLS

TECHNIQUE 1

TECHNIQUE 2

NOTES

DATE: _____ **WEEK:** _____ **HOURS TRAINED:** _____

INSTRUCTOR: _____ **TIME:** _____

GOALS

WARM UP/ DRILLS

TECHNIQUE 1

TECHNIQUE 2

NOTES

DATE: [ ]　　**WEEK:** [ ]　　**HOURS TRAINED:** [ ]

INSTRUCTOR: [ ]　　**TIME:** [ ]

GOALS

WARM UP/ DRILLS

TECHNIQUE 1

TECHNIQUE 2

NOTES

DATE: [ ] **WEEK:** [ ] **HOURS TRAINED:** [ ]

INSTRUCTOR: [ ] **TIME:** [ ]

GOALS

WARM UP/ DRILLS

TECHNIQUE 1

TECHNIQUE 2

NOTES

DATE: [ ] **WEEK:** [ ] **HOURS TRAINED:** [ ]

INSTRUCTOR: [ ] **TIME:** [ ]

GOALS

WARM UP/ DRILLS

TECHNIQUE 1

TECHNIQUE 2

NOTES

DATE: _____ **WEEK:** _____ **HOURS TRAINED:** _____

INSTRUCTOR: _____ **TIME:** _____

GOALS

WARM UP/ DRILLS

TECHNIQUE 1

TECHNIQUE 2

NOTES

DATE: _____ **WEEK:** _____ **HOURS TRAINED:** _____

INSTRUCTOR: _____ **TIME:** _____

GOALS

WARM UP/ DRILLS

TECHNIQUE 1

TECHNIQUE 2

NOTES

DATE: **WEEK:** **HOURS TRAINED:**

INSTRUCTOR: **TIME:**

GOALS

WARM UP/ DRILLS

TECHNIQUE 1

TECHNIQUE 2

NOTES

DATE: **WEEK:**   **HOURS TRAINED:**

INSTRUCTOR: **TIME:**

GOALS

WARM UP/ DRILLS

TECHNIQUE 1

TECHNIQUE 2

NOTES

DATE: **WEEK:** **HOURS TRAINED:**

INSTRUCTOR: **TIME:**

GOALS

WARM UP/ DRILLS

TECHNIQUE 1

TECHNIQUE 2

NOTES

DATE:		WEEK:		HOURS TRAINED:	
INSTRUCTOR:				TIME:	

GOALS

WARM UP/ DRILLS

TECHNIQUE 1

TECHNIQUE 2

NOTES

DATE: [ ] **WEEK:** [ ] **HOURS TRAINED:** [ ]

INSTRUCTOR: [ ] **TIME:** [ ]

GOALS

WARM UP/ DRILLS

TECHNIQUE 1

TECHNIQUE 2

NOTES

DATE: **WEEK:** **HOURS TRAINED:**

INSTRUCTOR: **TIME:**

GOALS

WARM UP/ DRILLS

TECHNIQUE 1

TECHNIQUE 2

NOTES

DATE: **WEEK:**   **HOURS TRAINED:**

INSTRUCTOR: **TIME:**

GOALS

WARM UP/ DRILLS

TECHNIQUE 1

TECHNIQUE 2

NOTES

DATE:		WEEK:		HOURS TRAINED:	
INSTRUCTOR:				TIME:	

GOALS

WARM UP/ DRILLS

TECHNIQUE 1

TECHNIQUE 2

NOTES

DATE: [   ] **WEEK:** [   ] **HOURS TRAINED:** [   ]

INSTRUCTOR: [   ] **TIME:** [   ]

GOALS

WARM UP/ DRILLS

TECHNIQUE 1

TECHNIQUE 2

NOTES

DATE: _____ **WEEK:** _____ **HOURS TRAINED:** _____

INSTRUCTOR: _____ **TIME:** _____

GOALS

WARM UP/ DRILLS

TECHNIQUE 1

TECHNIQUE 2

NOTES

DATE: **WEEK:**   **HOURS TRAINED:**

INSTRUCTOR: **TIME:**

GOALS

WARM UP/ DRILLS

TECHNIQUE 1

TECHNIQUE 2

NOTES

DATE: | **WEEK:** | **HOURS TRAINED:**

INSTRUCTOR: | **TIME:**

GOALS

WARM UP/ DRILLS

TECHNIQUE 1

TECHNIQUE 2

NOTES

DATE: | **WEEK:** | **HOURS TRAINED:**

INSTRUCTOR: | **TIME:**

GOALS

WARM UP/ DRILLS

TECHNIQUE 1

TECHNIQUE 2

NOTES

DATE: _____ **WEEK:** _____ **HOURS TRAINED:** _____

INSTRUCTOR: _____ **TIME:** _____

GOALS

WARM UP/ DRILLS

TECHNIQUE 1

TECHNIQUE 2

NOTES

DATE: | **WEEK:** | **HOURS TRAINED:**

INSTRUCTOR: | **TIME:**

GOALS

WARM UP/ DRILLS

TECHNIQUE 1

TECHNIQUE 2

NOTES

DATE: _____ **WEEK:** _____ **HOURS TRAINED:** _____

INSTRUCTOR: _____ **TIME:** _____

GOALS

WARM UP/ DRILLS

TECHNIQUE 1

TECHNIQUE 2

NOTES

DATE: **WEEK:**   **HOURS TRAINED:**

INSTRUCTOR: **TIME:**

GOALS

WARM UP/ DRILLS

TECHNIQUE 1

TECHNIQUE 2

NOTES

DATE: **WEEK:**   **HOURS TRAINED:**

INSTRUCTOR: **TIME:**

GOALS

WARM UP/ DRILLS

TECHNIQUE 1

TECHNIQUE 2

NOTES

DATE: **WEEK:**   **HOURS TRAINED:**

INSTRUCTOR: **TIME:**

GOALS

WARM UP/ DRILLS

TECHNIQUE 1

TECHNIQUE 2

NOTES

DATE:		WEEK:		HOURS TRAINED:	
INSTRUCTOR:				TIME:	

GOALS

WARM UP/ DRILLS

TECHNIQUE 1

TECHNIQUE 2

NOTES

DATE: **WEEK:**   **HOURS TRAINED:**

INSTRUCTOR: **TIME:**

GOALS

WARM UP/ DRILLS

TECHNIQUE 1

TECHNIQUE 2

NOTES

DATE: [_____] **WEEK:** [___] **HOURS TRAINED:** [_____]

INSTRUCTOR: [_____] **TIME:** [_____]

GOALS

WARM UP/ DRILLS

TECHNIQUE 1

TECHNIQUE 2

NOTES

DATE: _____ **WEEK:** _____ **HOURS TRAINED:** _____

INSTRUCTOR: _____ **TIME:** _____

GOALS

WARM UP/ DRILLS

TECHNIQUE 1

TECHNIQUE 2

NOTES

DATE: **WEEK:** **HOURS TRAINED:**

INSTRUCTOR: **TIME:**

GOALS

WARM UP/ DRILLS

TECHNIQUE 1

TECHNIQUE 2

NOTES

DATE: **WEEK:** **HOURS TRAINED:**

INSTRUCTOR: **TIME:**

GOALS

WARM UP/ DRILLS

TECHNIQUE 1

TECHNIQUE 2

NOTES

DATE: | **WEEK:** | **HOURS TRAINED:**

INSTRUCTOR: | **TIME:**

GOALS

WARM UP/ DRILLS

TECHNIQUE 1

TECHNIQUE 2

NOTES

DATE: **WEEK:**   **HOURS TRAINED:**

INSTRUCTOR: **TIME:**

GOALS

WARM UP/ DRILLS

TECHNIQUE 1

TECHNIQUE 2

NOTES

DATE: **WEEK:**   **HOURS TRAINED:**

INSTRUCTOR: **TIME:**

GOALS

WARM UP/ DRILLS

TECHNIQUE 1

TECHNIQUE 2

NOTES

DATE: | **WEEK:** | **HOURS TRAINED:**

INSTRUCTOR: | **TIME:**

GOALS

WARM UP/ DRILLS

TECHNIQUE 1

TECHNIQUE 2

NOTES

DATE: **WEEK:**   **HOURS TRAINED:**

INSTRUCTOR: **TIME:**

GOALS

WARM UP/ DRILLS

TECHNIQUE 1

TECHNIQUE 2

NOTES

DATE: [ ]   **WEEK:** [ ]   **HOURS TRAINED:** [ ]

INSTRUCTOR: [ ]   **TIME:** [ ]

GOALS

WARM UP/ DRILLS

TECHNIQUE 1

TECHNIQUE 2

NOTES

DATE: **WEEK:** **HOURS TRAINED:**

INSTRUCTOR: **TIME:**

GOALS

WARM UP/ DRILLS

TECHNIQUE 1

TECHNIQUE 2

NOTES

DATE: _____ **WEEK:** _____ **HOURS TRAINED:** _____

INSTRUCTOR: _____ **TIME:** _____

GOALS

WARM UP/ DRILLS

TECHNIQUE 1

TECHNIQUE 2

NOTES

DATE: _____ **WEEK:** _____ **HOURS TRAINED:** _____

INSTRUCTOR: _____ **TIME:** _____

GOALS

WARM UP/ DRILLS

TECHNIQUE 1

TECHNIQUE 2

NOTES

DATE: **WEEK:** **HOURS TRAINED:**

INSTRUCTOR: **TIME:**

GOALS

WARM UP/ DRILLS

TECHNIQUE 1

TECHNIQUE 2

NOTES

DATE:		WEEK:		HOURS TRAINED:	
INSTRUCTOR:				TIME:	

GOALS

WARM UP/ DRILLS

TECHNIQUE 1

TECHNIQUE 2

NOTES

DATE: **WEEK:** **HOURS TRAINED:**

INSTRUCTOR: **TIME:**

GOALS

WARM UP/ DRILLS

TECHNIQUE 1

TECHNIQUE 2

NOTES

DATE: | **WEEK:** | **HOURS TRAINED:**

INSTRUCTOR: | **TIME:**

GOALS

WARM UP/ DRILLS

TECHNIQUE 1

TECHNIQUE 2

NOTES

DATE: _____ **WEEK:** _____ **HOURS TRAINED:** _____

INSTRUCTOR: _____ **TIME:** _____

GOALS

WARM UP/ DRILLS

TECHNIQUE 1

TECHNIQUE 2

NOTES

DATE:		WEEK:		HOURS TRAINED:	

INSTRUCTOR: TIME:

GOALS

WARM UP/ DRILLS

TECHNIQUE 1

TECHNIQUE 2

NOTES

DATE: _____ **WEEK:** _____ **HOURS TRAINED:** _____

INSTRUCTOR: _____ **TIME:** _____

GOALS

WARM UP/ DRILLS

TECHNIQUE 1

TECHNIQUE 2

NOTES

DATE: **WEEK:**   **HOURS TRAINED:**

INSTRUCTOR: **TIME:**

GOALS

WARM UP/ DRILLS

TECHNIQUE 1

TECHNIQUE 2

NOTES

DATE: **WEEK:**   **HOURS TRAINED:**

INSTRUCTOR: **TIME:**

GOALS

WARM UP/ DRILLS

TECHNIQUE 1

TECHNIQUE 2

NOTES

DATE: [   ]   **WEEK:** [   ]   **HOURS TRAINED:** [   ]

INSTRUCTOR: [   ]   **TIME:** [   ]

GOALS

WARM UP/ DRILLS

TECHNIQUE 1

TECHNIQUE 2

NOTES

DATE: _____ **WEEK:** _____ **HOURS TRAINED:** _____

INSTRUCTOR: _____ **TIME:** _____

GOALS

WARM UP/ DRILLS

TECHNIQUE 1

TECHNIQUE 2

NOTES

DATE: [   ]   **WEEK:** [   ]   **HOURS TRAINED:** [   ]

INSTRUCTOR: [   ]   **TIME:** [   ]

GOALS

WARM UP/ DRILLS

TECHNIQUE 1

TECHNIQUE 2

NOTES

DATE: **WEEK:**   **HOURS TRAINED:**

INSTRUCTOR: **TIME:**

GOALS

WARM UP/ DRILLS

TECHNIQUE 1

TECHNIQUE 2

NOTES

DATE:		WEEK:		HOURS TRAINED:	
INSTRUCTOR:				TIME:	

GOALS

WARM UP/ DRILLS

TECHNIQUE 1

TECHNIQUE 2

NOTES

DATE: | **WEEK:** | **HOURS TRAINED:**

INSTRUCTOR: | **TIME:**

GOALS

WARM UP/ DRILLS

TECHNIQUE 1

TECHNIQUE 2

NOTES

DATE: [   ] **WEEK:** [   ] **HOURS TRAINED:** [   ]

INSTRUCTOR: [   ] **TIME:** [   ]

GOALS

WARM UP/ DRILLS

TECHNIQUE 1

TECHNIQUE 2

NOTES

DATE: _____ **WEEK:** _____ **HOURS TRAINED:** _____

INSTRUCTOR: _____ **TIME:** _____

GOALS

WARM UP/ DRILLS

TECHNIQUE 1

TECHNIQUE 2

NOTES

DATE: _____ **WEEK:** _____ **HOURS TRAINED:** _____

INSTRUCTOR: _____ **TIME:** _____

GOALS

WARM UP/ DRILLS

TECHNIQUE 1

TECHNIQUE 2

NOTES

DATE: _____ **WEEK:** _____ **HOURS TRAINED:** _____

INSTRUCTOR: _____ **TIME:** _____

GOALS

WARM UP/ DRILLS

TECHNIQUE 1

TECHNIQUE 2

NOTES

DATE: _____ **WEEK:** _____ **HOURS TRAINED:** _____

INSTRUCTOR: _____ **TIME:** _____

GOALS

WARM UP/ DRILLS

TECHNIQUE 1

TECHNIQUE 2

NOTES

DATE: **WEEK:**   **HOURS TRAINED:**

INSTRUCTOR: **TIME:**

GOALS

WARM UP/ DRILLS

TECHNIQUE 1

TECHNIQUE 2

NOTES

DATE: | **WEEK:** | **HOURS TRAINED:**

INSTRUCTOR: | **TIME:**

GOALS

WARM UP/ DRILLS

TECHNIQUE 1

TECHNIQUE 2

NOTES

DATE: **WEEK:** **HOURS TRAINED:**

INSTRUCTOR: **TIME:**

GOALS

WARM UP/ DRILLS

TECHNIQUE 1

TECHNIQUE 2

NOTES

DATE: _____ **WEEK:** _____ **HOURS TRAINED:** _____

INSTRUCTOR: _____ **TIME:** _____

GOALS

WARM UP/ DRILLS

TECHNIQUE 1

TECHNIQUE 2

NOTES

DATE: **WEEK:** **HOURS TRAINED:**

INSTRUCTOR: **TIME:**

GOALS

WARM UP/ DRILLS

TECHNIQUE 1

TECHNIQUE 2

NOTES

DATE: _____ **WEEK:** _____ **HOURS TRAINED:** _____

INSTRUCTOR: _____ **TIME:** _____

GOALS

WARM UP/ DRILLS

TECHNIQUE 1

TECHNIQUE 2

NOTES

DATE: **WEEK:**   **HOURS TRAINED:**

INSTRUCTOR: **TIME:**

GOALS

WARM UP/ DRILLS

TECHNIQUE 1

TECHNIQUE 2

NOTES

DATE: **WEEK:**   **HOURS TRAINED:**

INSTRUCTOR: **TIME:**

GOALS

WARM UP/ DRILLS

TECHNIQUE 1

TECHNIQUE 2

NOTES

DATE: [   ]   **WEEK:** [   ]   **HOURS TRAINED:** [   ]

INSTRUCTOR: [   ]   **TIME:** [   ]

GOALS

WARM UP/ DRILLS

TECHNIQUE 1

TECHNIQUE 2

NOTES

DATE: **WEEK:** **HOURS TRAINED:**

INSTRUCTOR: **TIME:**

GOALS

WARM UP/ DRILLS

TECHNIQUE 1

TECHNIQUE 2

NOTES

DATE: **WEEK:**   **HOURS TRAINED:**

INSTRUCTOR: **TIME:**

GOALS

WARM UP/ DRILLS

TECHNIQUE 1

TECHNIQUE 2

NOTES

DATE: _____ **WEEK:** ____ **HOURS TRAINED:** _____

INSTRUCTOR: _____ **TIME:** _____

GOALS

WARM UP/ DRILLS

TECHNIQUE 1

TECHNIQUE 2

NOTES

DATE: **WEEK:** **HOURS TRAINED:**

INSTRUCTOR: **TIME:**

GOALS

WARM UP/ DRILLS

TECHNIQUE 1

TECHNIQUE 2

NOTES

DATE:		WEEK:		HOURS TRAINED:	

INSTRUCTOR:		TIME:	

GOALS

WARM UP/ DRILLS

TECHNIQUE 1

TECHNIQUE 2

NOTES

DATE: **WEEK:** **HOURS TRAINED:**

INSTRUCTOR: **TIME:**

GOALS

WARM UP/ DRILLS

TECHNIQUE 1

TECHNIQUE 2

NOTES

DATE: _____ **WEEK:** ___ **HOURS TRAINED:** _____

INSTRUCTOR: _____ **TIME:** _____

GOALS

WARM UP/ DRILLS

TECHNIQUE 1

TECHNIQUE 2

NOTES

DATE: **WEEK:**   **HOURS TRAINED:**

INSTRUCTOR: **TIME:**

GOALS

WARM UP/ DRILLS

TECHNIQUE 1

TECHNIQUE 2

NOTES

DATE: _____ **WEEK:** _____ **HOURS TRAINED:** _____

INSTRUCTOR: _____ **TIME:** _____

GOALS

WARM UP/ DRILLS

TECHNIQUE 1

TECHNIQUE 2

NOTES

DATE: **WEEK:**   **HOURS TRAINED:**

INSTRUCTOR: **TIME:**

GOALS

WARM UP/ DRILLS

TECHNIQUE 1

TECHNIQUE 2

NOTES

DATE: [   ]   **WEEK:** [   ]   **HOURS TRAINED:** [   ]

INSTRUCTOR: [   ]   **TIME:** [   ]

GOALS

WARM UP/ DRILLS

TECHNIQUE 1

TECHNIQUE 2

NOTES

DATE: _____ **WEEK:** _____ **HOURS TRAINED:** _____

INSTRUCTOR: _____ **TIME:** _____

GOALS

WARM UP/ DRILLS

TECHNIQUE 1

TECHNIQUE 2

NOTES

DATE: ☐ **WEEK:** ☐ **HOURS TRAINED:** ☐

INSTRUCTOR: ☐ **TIME:** ☐

GOALS

WARM UP/ DRILLS

TECHNIQUE 1

TECHNIQUE 2

NOTES

CPSIA information can be obtained
at www.ICGtesting.com
Printed in the USA
BVHW040043070420
577065BV00007B/135

9 781729 633205